THROUGH THEIR EYES

FRAGMENTS OF FOREVER

Edited By Lynsey Evans

First published in Great Britain in 2024 by:

Young Writers
Remus House
Coltsfoot Drive
Peterborough
PE2 9BF
Telephone: 01733 890066
Website: www.youngwriters.co.uk

All Rights Reserved
Book Design by Ashley Janson
© Copyright Contributors 2024
Softback ISBN 978-1-83565-806-2
Printed and bound in the UK by BookPrintingUK
Website: www.bookprintinguk.com
YB0606K

FOREWORD

Since 1991, here at Young Writers we have celebrated the awesome power of creative writing, especially in young adults, where it can serve as a vital method of expressing strong (and sometimes difficult) emotions, a conduit to develop empathy, and a safe, non-judgemental place to explore one's own place in the world. With every poem we see the effort and thought that each pupil published in this book has put into their work and by creating this anthology we hope to encourage them further with the ultimate goal of sparking a life-long love of writing.

Through Their Eyes challenged young writers to open their minds and pen bold, powerful poems from the points-of-view of any person or concept they could imagine – from celebrities and politicians to animals and inanimate objects, or even just to give us a glimpse of the world as they experience it. The result is this fierce collection of poetry that by turns questions injustice, imagines the innermost thoughts of influential figures or simply has fun.

The nature of the topic means that contentious or controversial figures may have been chosen as the narrators, and as such some poems may contain views or thoughts that, although may represent those of the person being written about, by no means reflect the opinions or feelings of either the author or us here at Young Writers.

We encourage young writers to express themselves and address subjects that matter to them, which sometimes means writing about sensitive or difficult topics. If you have been affected by any issues raised in this book, details on where to find help can be found at
www.youngwriters.co.uk/contact-lines

CONTENTS

Ernest Bevin Academy, Tooting

Pratharshan Janarththanan (14)	1
Umar Shakhawath (12)	2
Anas Khan (12)	4
Yahya Khan (12)	5
Muhammad Ibrahim Hussain (12)	6
Hussein Moussa (13)	7
Abdulbasid Muse (14)	8
Mjnari Carty Sai	9
Yahya Farhat (12)	10
Spencer Aviso-Grigorey (14)	12
Tirth Patel (14)	13
Tyler Chin (12)	14
Freddie Cox (14)	15
Nayan Patel (14)	16
Elijah Simms-Alder	17
Abu-Baur Meskin (13)	18
Abdullah Khan (13)	19
Muhammad Ibrahim (12)	20
Timofei Gaiduc (12)	21
Veer Patel (14)	22
Hudaifah Patel (12)	23
Ilyas Corneh (12)	24
Kyran Scott (13)	25
Josiah Mbeledogu (13)	26
Rayyan Khurram (13)	27
Adam Mahmed (12)	28
Cheyenne Fernandes (11)	29
Robin Concepcion (13)	30
Samuel Kilby (11)	31
Deniro Daley (13)	32
Ryad Muir (13)	33
Mohammed Qureshi (13)	34
Jibril Abdul Wahab (13)	35
Danyaal Ali (13)	36

Kevin Catano (13)	37

Flint High School, Flint

Amilee Williams (14)	38
Victor Dziura (14)	40
Alice Elliott (15)	41
Ffion Lucking (13)	42
Mia Davies (12)	44
Macey Bowden (13)	45
Fearne Conway (13)	46
Jacob Gordon (13)	47
Seren Conway (13)	48
Seren Thompson (12)	50
Rhys Messiter (11)	51
Lila Grace Jordens (12)	52
Angel Williams (12)	53
Savio Costa (13)	54
Antonia Moise (12)	55
Lloyd Wilkes (13)	56
Lexi-Ann O'Brien	57
Ethan Williams (14)	58
Scarlett Thompson (12)	59
Cerys Holt (11)	60
Dylan Jones (23)	61
Ryan Gittins (13)	62
Muhib Ansari	63
Lexie Butcher (13)	64
Nancy Wilson (13)	65
Eva Jones (12)	66
Carys Fion Williams (12)	67
Maizie Jones (13)	68
Kian Taylor (14)	69
Evie Ross (13)	70
Flynn Osborne (12)	71
Efe Igbinoba (14)	72

Adam Mrlina (12)	73
Hannah Squire (12)	74
Osian Jones (14)	75
Anna Austin (12)	76
Kendal Cohen (11)	77
Keeva Beck (12)	78
Jack Collins (12)	79
Kacey-Leigh Jones (13) & Katie	80
Brody Duncan (13)	81
Riley Smith (13)	82
Olivia Marsh (12)	83
Emily Seddon (12)	84
Thomas Latham (12)	85
Darcel Jones (12)	86
Chelsea Collo (12)	87
Olivia Owens (11)	88
Lola Hammersley (11)	89
Caelan Acott (13)	90
Ruby Cowden (11)	91
Juliet Lewis	92
Hollie Warburton	93
Frankie Price	94
Lexi-May Sebrina McCarron (12)	95
Mia Brown (12)	96
Keira Newton (12)	97
Finley Russell (13)	98
Calvin Peters (11)	99
Luis Griffith (12)	100
Callum Harding (12)	101
Sophia Jones (11)	102
Leon Croll (12)	103
Nia-Jane Hinds (13)	104
Olivia Marsh (12)	105
Carla Showell (12)	106
Anthony Smith (12)	107
Ryan Lally (12)	108
Ethan Thomas (12)	109
Grace Jones (13)	110
Evie Hale (12)	111
Penelope Ann Machell (11)	112
Millie Roberts (13)	113
Alex Doran (12)	114

Gloucester Academy, Gloucester

Martha Neininger (12)	115
Joanna Rajah (11)	116
Edward Williamson-Giles (12)	117
George Brooksbank-Hardacre (12)	118
Riley Holpin (12)	119
Luke Butt (12)	120
Martha Jones (12)	121
Aaliyah Knights (11)	122

Maple Medical PRU, Balby

Kairon Booker (13)	123
Kian Flint (14)	124
Mia Martin (14)	125
Evie Lakin (12)	126
Sian Machin (14)	127
Brooke Woodward (13)	128

THE POEMS

Consequences

Why do I have to swim through this every day?
As I swim through this, I feel pain,
As I swim past my family, I cry,
As I see plastic dancing around, I feel pain,
As the place to go to decrease, I cry,
As there's no food, I feel pain,
As my friends say goodbye, I cry,
As the population of humans increase, I feel pain,
As I swim as far as possible, I still cry,
As no one is doing anything, I feel pain,
As all the species go extinct, I cry,
As tides increase and decrease, I still feel pain,
Will I ever feel normal again?
Will I finally stop saying goodbye to my friends?
When will you make a change?
When will I get a proper place to live?
What will humans do?
What will happen next?
It's time to make a change!

Pratharshan Janarththanan (14)
Ernest Bevin Academy, Tooting

Free Palestine

Oh, people of Gaza,
We hear your cries,
In which the world leaders have denied.

Newborn babies have just been born,
Sadly, they have never seen dawn.

Self-defence has been used,
By Israel
From a country to hide away,
From rocks.
How could it be justified -
When innocents die from bombs?

Helpless children,
That don't have support!
The world leaders have been quiet,
All they have left is hope.

As we cherish, they perish,
Some wonder and ponder,
If they can live another day...

As the world leaders watch
Palestine crumble,
Has Israel ever been humble?
Why are the world leaders blind?
When genocide enters occupiers' mind...

From the river to the sea
Palestine will be free...
Palestine will be free...

Umar Shakhawath (12)
Ernest Bevin Academy, Tooting

Free Palestine!

I pray for Palestine that they will be free!
I hear the babies crying and children
I hear the sirens of the ambulance going place to place.
I see people dying while Israel start bombing Palestine
Will the world stand up for Palestine?
I hear the rumble of my tummy while I stand hungry.
I taste the metallic blood of myself and fight back!
The innocent lives of Gaza die and leave their souls
Babies and children upset and crying, saying,
"Why did my parents leave me?"
"I can't live without my parents."
"Palestine will be free In sha Allah."
"Palestine will be free In sha Allah."
"Free, free Palestine."
"Free, free Palestine."

Anas Khan (12)
Ernest Bevin Academy, Tooting

Did You Have To Persecute Them?

Me and my older brother are the only ones left.
My mum and dad are the ones who are dead.
There's a genocide in my country,
We cry too, all the Allied countries are in sorrow too.
Parents mourning loss, news warning of a terrorist in a mosque
The genocide in Germany, World War II,
Everyone helped but when it's Palestine,
Apparently, 'there is nothing you can do'.
Bombs falling like endless rain,
There's nothing to stop unbearable pain.
Please just stop the unbearable pain.
A homeless Palestinian boy knocks on my door and begs for food.
I ask him, "Who did this to you?"
"They did it to my friends and family too!"
Stop the genocide!

Yahya Khan (12)
Ernest Bevin Academy, Tooting

Terror Of Tremor And Life Of Betrayed Youth

Since the bullets are rampaging from each rattle of shells
fallen from the sky as wailing bells,
only left, buildings of devastation.
They revive lies into the truth,
while their heart tenders into materials of air
filled with innocence
now wisps of white vapour evade the surface and skies.
We wished in our hearts
in our desire
while the crestfallen many die in their slumber
and the charging show no mercy
in their bitter safety, they awake alone
as homeless.
Where is the peace of times
that began to make their hearts so sluggish?
Only the lithium smells and tastes on their skin to embrace
and the deadly silence of ash into terror.

Muhammad Ibrahim Hussain (12)
Ernest Bevin Academy, Tooting

Criminal's Life

"Criminal, criminal, criminal!" That's the only words I hear wherever I walk
From whomever I seek
I am always judged for killing a man
But people don't know the truth of this story
"It wasn't my fault!" I scream
But they don't believe me.

I was walking down the street late at night
A man jumped out
He tried to rob me
I had a gun but so did he
Bang! There was a shout, there was a scream
People's lights turned on, so I had to flee

I killed him, I killed him
But it wasn't my fault
I was caught and now I am waiting to take my last breath.

Hussein Moussa (13)
Ernest Bevin Academy, Tooting

Through The Eyes Of A Blind Man

A man that is blind,
Cannot see much,
All their eyes see is darkness,
Which could never be fun.

A blind man is quite cheerful
And happy all around,
But we wouldn't stop and think,
What is it like to see black clouds?

A blind man's hearing,
Can be very great,
He can even hear the mouse speaking,
Below the grate.

The blind man's nose
Is very good
It could even smell the bad stench,
From the mole down below.

So next time you see a blind man,
Don't let your thoughts be hasty,
As blind men's qualities are dainty.

Abdulbasid Muse (14)
Ernest Bevin Academy, Tooting

Freedom and Pain

The word freedom,
One meaning untied,
Unchained and alive,
That is the word, freedom.

Freedom,
Seen in dreams and eyes,
But they're restrained and detained,
That is a dream of freedom.

Freedom,
A piece of will,
Taken and controlled,
That is colonisation.

Freedom,
Taken from generation to generation,
Spread from nation to nation,
Taken and taken,
But be not mistaken,
That this freedom can't be obtained,
As people who are free are great,
And those who are not,
Filled with disdain,
Pain.

Mjnari Carty Sai
Ernest Bevin Academy, Tooting

The Dead Kids

If I shall die,
You shall live,
To tell the tale,
Of the dead kids.

Bombs drop,
My ringing ears,
No time to stop,
Just look at my dead peers.

If I shall die,
You shall live,
To tell the tale,
Of the dead kids.

A prison for all,
No one can leave,
A child's call,
And then he grieves.

If I shall die,
You shall live,
To tell the tale,
Of the dead kids.

What hatred is held in hearts,
When parents bury body parts,
Surrounded by so much death,
Any moment could be my last breath.

Yahya Farhat (12)
Ernest Bevin Academy, Tooting

A World On Fire

Dirt, smoke and heat.
Let's get our priorities straight.
If not, generations to come are as good as done
And the chance of survival is none.
The world is engulfed in flames and so nearly are we too.
We must try and do something now.
Sustainability. It's a start. After all, it only takes a few.
People will follow, then follow then follow.
Do your best not to make this promise hollow.
Today is better than never,
So let's try to be clever,
Change now or regret forever.
Time to make a change now,
Whilst the time still does allow.

Spencer Aviso-Grigorey (14)
Ernest Bevin Academy, Tooting

Be Grateful

In our eyes, we see an apple,
But through their eyes, they see a salad.
In our eyes, we see a piece of cardboard,
But through their eyes, they see a bed.

Some people wish to be in the position
That you are in right now.

In our eyes, we see a pet,
But through their eyes, they see a best friend.
In our eyes, we see scrap,
But through their eyes, they see shelter.

Some people would do ridiculous things,
To have the same possessions as you.
Many people aren't as lucky as you are,
So be grateful for what you have.

Tirth Patel (14)
Ernest Bevin Academy, Tooting

Not Everything Is As It Seems

A young boy alone, afraid.
Perhaps seen as brave and fearless.
Everything is not how it seems.

Young powerful woman, both smart and strong,
Feels weak, powerless, out of control.
Everything is not how it looks.

People around the world, any gender,
Lie with happy faces.
Feel within themselves that they have to hide their feelings.
Themselves.
Feelings aren't something you can see.

Look around you.
People you don't know.
Strangers looking confident, with their heads held high.
But you don't know what they feel,
What they think, or imagine.

Everything is not as it seems.

Tyler Chin (12)
Ernest Bevin Academy, Tooting

The Attack

I lie on the soft mud,
Licking my taste buds,
Ready for the massacre at hand,
With my armed and scary band,
We await our prey, like we are wolves,
Little do we know, we are fools,
Iron and gunpowder drains the sky,
As my family and comrades say, "Goodbye!"
I run across the trenches, holding my friend,
I didn't know it was already his end,
I drop him at the sight of it all,
I have been shot, so I fall,
I cry, knowing this is never going to stop,
And I'm going to be remembered on a rigid, rancid rock.

Freddie Cox (14)
Ernest Bevin Academy, Tooting

Is There Something Wrong With Me?

Is there something wrong with me?
I obsess on the opportunity,
To put others back together,
So much so, that gradually,
I let go of myself,
Forgetting myself...
I keep walking forward,
Leaving my heart behind me,
A strange pit left on my chest,
An emptiness to fill.

Maybe pulling myself under their emotions,
Allows me to cope with mine,
Soften the burden,
Yet for some reason,
I cling onto the ghost of myself,
Giving up on recovery,
I think there's something wrong with me...

Nayan Patel (14)
Ernest Bevin Academy, Tooting

The Monster Under My Bed

The monster under my bed,
He might cut off my head,
He comes out at night,
I'm prepared to fight,
The monster under my bed.

The monster under my bed,
He's ready to be fed,
His claws as sharp as flint,
His breath needs some mint,
The monster under my bed.

The monster under my bed,
"Come out, come out," he said,
His blazing red eyes,
Either me or him who dies,
The monster under the bed.

The monster under my bed,
Turns out I'm dead.

Elijah Simms-Alder
Ernest Bevin Academy, Tooting

A Day To Woe

If you ever feel,
Like you can never heal,
You always have a place to go,
For there is no use for woe.

Come here,
For we can shield you from your fear,
As this day, this day of woe,
Shall come forth with a stupendous flow,
Hold on to your mother,
It may be the last time she can bother,
For this day may bring,
The darkest thing.

He will come,
It won't be fun,
For he shall be here,
The epitome of fear,
The death bringer,
Oh,
About a day to woe.

Abu-Baur Meskin (13)
Ernest Bevin Academy, Tooting

My Idol, Kobbie Mainoo

K ing of Manchester when he plays.
O utstanding vision when he passes,
B rilliant ball control when he dribbles,
B right youngster for England.
I nternational sensation for Manchester United.
E xceeding expectations for everyone.

M asterclass finishing, you cannot stop him,
A mazing defending, you can't get past him.
I nternet sensation, everyone loving him.
N o one can stop this man.
O utrageous skills when he's on the ball,
O ut-of-this-world type of player.

Abdullah Khan (13)
Ernest Bevin Academy, Tooting

Freedom

F reedom, a sweet luxury those so fortunate don't gain,
R ampaging, heartless, genocide comes and raids,
'E thnic cleanser' disturbs serenity with horror under its reign,
E veryone who had freedom watches them fade,
D readful colonies take and plunder,
O utrageous like Vikings, shoot and fire,
M eanwhile, those who have freedom, watch as they don't accept surrender as I speak on behalf of those who don't achieve freedom from a ceasefire.

Muhammad Ibrahim (12)
Ernest Bevin Academy, Tooting

I Am A Soldier

People think war is fun and games,
When truly, it's eternal pain,
Hearing the screams of people,
Makes my face turn blue,
Knowing there's nothing I can do.

People think after war is over, everything is okay,
But it feels like everything has just turned grey,
Walking on a street and I hear something loud,
My stomach turns around,
War is serious and we should respect the people
Who fought in the wars,
War is not a joke,
I am a soldier.

Timofei Gaiduc (12)
Ernest Bevin Academy, Tooting

Refugees

R eady to live like a normal child again
E scaping what once was his home
F rightened of what is to come
U pcoming challenges no one will understand
G etting ready to begin a new chapter
E ating less than usual, trying to survive
E quality is the dream
S oon to be a normal child again

Ready to live in a home
Make new friends
Start a new education
Build from the ground to the clouds.

Veer Patel (14)
Ernest Bevin Academy, Tooting

Palestine

Everybody knows this one state,
Being killed, is the civilians' fate.
The media dressing it up, lying,
People here are dying.
The water, gas and electricity access is denied,
Too many innocent people have died.
Everyone please let them live,
There is always something you can give.

It's called peace

Peace for the people of Gaza, who need,
Equality, freedom and human rights.

Hudaifah Patel (12)
Ernest Bevin Academy, Tooting

War Sense

I can feel the ground rumble,
My heart's no longer soft,
I can hear my friends cry,
For the people we have lost,
I can taste betrayal from the UN,
And the metallic taste of blood,
I can smell my mum's cooking,
As I pray for Palestine,
I can tell my mum is crying,
As all the deaths still hurt my mind,
I just know my stomach hurts,
And I ask, please free Palestine.

Ilyas Corneh (12)
Ernest Bevin Academy, Tooting

The Mind Of A Soldier

The mind of a soldier is very complex,
The bangs, the screams, the horror, the death.

Day after day, my comrades lie hurt,
The bones, the blood, their bodies all burned,
The crackle of rifles as the enemies approach,
No one to save me, this war is a hoax,
Not one night of sleep, I sit and weep,
Still waiting for death to return,

All of this trouble and what do I earn?

Kyran Scott (13)
Ernest Bevin Academy, Tooting

Through The Eyes Of A Son

I write with pride
As this one is dedicated to my mum
As a son
All the love that pumps through me
Goes to my mum
To make my mum proud
I go above and beyond

For a son to see their mum upset
It breaks their heart
At times you can't feel any emotion
You can't cry or laugh
Even when you see
Your mum shed a tear
Your happiness departs.

Josiah Mbeledogu (13)
Ernest Bevin Academy, Tooting

As The Sea I Guide You

As the sea, I say, don't litter in me,
As the sea, don't make me a bin,
As the sea, I don't want to die,
As the sea, I'm your main resource,
As the sea, my animals are becoming extinct,
Extinct because of you,
You don't think about us,
As the ocean, we all say, including the animals,
We need your help.

Help me (the ocean)!

Rayyan Khurram (13)
Ernest Bevin Academy, Tooting

A Refugee's Eyes

Guns roaring,
Death coming,
Bombs lie ahead,
Red covers my vision,
As I shake in fear,
TV shows turn into war and blood,
As houses crumble,
I finish packing as tears stream down my face,
Bodies surround my pitiful house
As bullets swipe past my head
There is no house anymore
We run, seeking bitter safety...

Adam Mahmed (12)
Ernest Bevin Academy, Tooting

As I

As I, Martin Luther King, I shall be,
The one that's petrified of it coming to me,
I am frightened that it has come,
I always wanted to give up, saying I am done.

As I sat down on my balcony every day,
I can't even think if it for one day,
Then I say to myself,
I shall do this for everybody else.

Cheyenne Fernandes (11)
Ernest Bevin Academy, Tooting

Home

You can throw trash at me
But I still provide you a home.
You can destroy me
Yet I still am your home.
My own tears will drown your land,
My heart will be set ablaze.
You say you will save me
Yet you are a scourge in my eyes.
Agony, suffering and sorrow,
My life wanes.
Yet I still am your home.
Why do you destroy me?
I am your home.

Robin Concepcion (13)
Ernest Bevin Academy, Tooting

My Ocean

I am a shark - king of the sea!
I swim to victory, but not anymore,
All I see is plastic waste and empty cans,
I am hungry, my food is either stuck in plastic or dead,
My beautiful sea, it's now destroyed,
All the good memories are now gone, my home is gone,

This place will never be the same!

Samuel Kilby (11)
Ernest Bevin Academy, Tooting

Messi

M agnificent
E xcellent
S hort king
S ignificant god
I ncredible

He's incredible, he's amazing,
He's Messi
Give me an M
Give me an E
Give me an S
Give me an S
Give me and I
What does that spell?
M-e-s-s-i.

Deniro Daley (13)
Ernest Bevin Academy, Tooting

The Life Of A Refugee

R efugees constantly flee.
E scaping from our homes to somewhere new.
F orced out of our land
U ndergoing horrible circumstances.
G oing to another country.
E nduring hardships.
E nding up in a tough spot.

This is the sad life of a refugee.

Ryad Muir (13)
Ernest Bevin Academy, Tooting

Phoenix

I am a bird that soars high in the sky,
My wings are flames that cover far and wide,
Each feather holds hope and dreams.
I am covered by ferocious flames,
The flames are strong.
Just like my name.
I am a phoenix,
That soars high in the sky to see another day.

Mohammed Qureshi (13)
Ernest Bevin Academy, Tooting

I Am A Criminal

I am a criminal,
I steal to live,
I steal to make a living,
I have to hide,
In order to thrive,
And once I'm near you,
You need to hide.

Jibril Abdul Wahab (13)
Ernest Bevin Academy, Tooting

Tree

T all and green,
R egularly seen,
E ndless little shoots,
E verlasting fruits.

Danyaal Ali (13)
Ernest Bevin Academy, Tooting

Life

Life can be unfair,
Life can be good,
Life can have faith that
Was once understood.

Kevin Catano (13)
Ernest Bevin Academy, Tooting

The Lonely Snowman

I look out the window and see my reflection
And through the fogged window in that direction
I see a snowman cold and alone
With no other snowmen and no snowman home

I would go outside to comfort him
But the bitter wind cannot come in
I long to go outside and build him a friend
But the blazing fire has no end

The snow falls like air
But the poor snowman looks full of despair
His carrot nose droops more and more
And all of a sudden it falls to the floor

That is it I can't watch for much longer
The wind is growing stronger and stronger
So I put on my coat, my hat and my boots
And I find a scarf or something that suits

I step outside and feel a chill
But the wind isn't as strong as my will
I wrap the scarf around his neck
And place a hat upon his head

With his carrot nose back in place
And a warm covering around his face
I go back inside and look out to the snow
And there sits the snowman his face all aglow.

Amilee Williams (14)
Flint High School, Flint

All In A Mouse's Night

The sun's gone down, the coast is clear,
Biscuit, the cat, seems to disappear.
The cheese cellar's open, so out of our cage, we come out.
Eyes locked on the door, no time to mess about.
We've prayed all day for the cat to sleep,
But just in case, we mustn't make a *peep*,
We rush out away across the floor,
To the open cellar door.
We take a long look inside and each pick out a cheese we like.
But as we turn towards our exits,
In the moonlight growls Biscuit,
With lizard eyes, he cuts our souls,
And his claws are out, ready to complete his role.
He charges at us at full speed,
A miracle to have is what we need.
And as Biscuit runs across in leaping bounds,
A block of cheese falls to the ground.
"Ouch!" the stupid cat exclaims,
With injured paws, he limps in pain,
What a tale, what a sight,
All inside a mouse's night!

Victor Dziura (14)
Flint High School, Flint

I Am A Therapist

I have seen it all.
I have seen pain, I have seen love, I have seen longing.
I have seen so much since the beginning.
I have seen the scars from the lives people have led.
I have seen the pressure put on people to find success.
I have seen people haunted by their harrowing pasts.
I have seen people fearful of what is to pass.
I have seen the power of regret.
I have seen the words they will never forget.
I have seen the weight of a timeless secret.
I have seen the relationships they have gripped.
I have seen the memories they have left.
I have seen the lives they have dreamt of.
I have seen their talents go to waste.
I have seen them try to find their place.
I have seen failure consume their minds.
I have seen the effects of mankind.
I have seen embodiments of grief.
I have seen people try to leave.

I am a therapist,
And it is my job to help and guide.

Alice Elliott (15)
Flint High School, Flint

Stop Trashing Our Oceans

Plastic is useful but it doesn't break down
It spends years and years lying around
Please
Please
Please
Please stop
Throwing rubbish in the sea
And just see that the animals just want to be free
In the ocean the plastic is deadly
And quite out of hand
It's now up to you to fix it
And make it sound
Fishes are eating these little pieces
And thinking it's their tea
I'm now being serious
This is not for me
If it's cold don't you shiver
You killer
And please
Please
Please
Please don't chuck litter in the river
We need to stop using plastic
Will you help me please?
It wraps around their necks
Their tails and their fins

Poor fish
So please
Please
Please
Please
Use less plastic
And think of this poem
Let's all save our oceans
And rivers, one piece at a time.

Ffion Lucking (13)
Flint High School, Flint

My Life As A Pet Dog

Chasing my ball, running down the hall,
I go out all day to have fun and play.
I eat all my dinner that's why I'm not any thinner,
When I'm on a walk I pick up a log.
After all, I'm a little dog.

I'm soft, round and full of fluff,
But sometimes I can also be tough.
Racing out of the house because I saw a cat bounce,
I always want cuddles after I've jumped in puddles.
I'll come with you to have a jog,
After all, I'm a little dog.

When I hear a noise I bark,
I pounce on you in the dark.
When I hop in front of you I make you trip,
I get scared when I hear a drip.
I'll roll on your new rug and chase a bug,
I still want to go out in the fog.
After all, I'm a little dog.

To my family I am loyal,
When my family is disrespected,
It makes my blood boil,
Sometimes, I'm not just a little dog.

Mia Davies (12)
Flint High School, Flint

Grief

I'm sorry that you're gone and now there's a grotesque monster in my stomach.
And now that you're gone it feels like I've just taken a bullet.
I can't leave my bed,
Because you pollute my head.
Memories flood in as I drown in images of your smile.
Am I in denial?
Just one last goodbye,
Did you have to die?
As my guilt consumes me,
My loneliness dooms me.
The sea of anguish that fills me,
It might as well just kill me.
At least then I can see you,
Then I can feel you.
Your warmth that fills my soul,
And your radiance, you would always glow.
Why you and not me?
God, couldn't you just let them be?
Am I always gonna feel this way?
I just wish that everything would go away!
They all call me grief,
Yet now, I plead for a sense of relief.

Macey Bowden (13)
Flint High School, Flint

The Heart Of A Soldier

I stand still and proud walking to the plane,
My blood pressure's high once again.
I suddenly realise it's time to say goodbye,
Goodbye to my family, goodbye to my friends.
As thoughts rush through my head, *will I ever return again?*
I worry for my regiment like I have once before.
What if they get injured in this terrible war?
This is so real now and I cannot flee,
Sometimes I wonder who will save little old me.
When I was small I thought a gun was a toy,
But I guess that was then, I now need to deploy.
I hear guns fire in the air,
I feel so bare like there's nothing there.
This is what my training's been for.
It's time to get out there and give it my all.
The fear, the hurt of skin and bone,
I'm alone at night,

I just want to come home.

Fearne Conway (13)
Flint High School, Flint

Through Our Eyes

At the start, we were confused about why they came (to our enormous island)
We didn't know what to do. Should we ask what they're doing here
Or should we let them do whatever they want to do?
Some of them were friendly, some of them weren't so much

Later, they came wrecking and destroying our homes and land
Stealing our furniture and everything we had in our homes
Thinking it was their island. They even began to kill some of us...
Our island was a complete mess

Devastated, the rabbits took over our land and our nature
Sadly, our island was destroyed. We couldn't fix it
We were vengeful, but annoyed they ran away
We wanted to take revenge and look for them and steal all our things that they stole from us.

Jacob Gordon (13)
Flint High School, Flint

The Terrific Story

I wake up
I'm feeling the power in my skin
Today's the big day,
And it's about to begin.

Then I amble in,
My heart is pounding,
I'm about to give in.

I'm up after Louis Smith,
My nerves are kicking,
It's happening now,
And it's about to begin.

I'm on the rings,
And doing my new trick,
And then...

I fall,
My life is flashing,
Then I land on my head.

My neck cracks,
I think I have died,
Then I can't stand,
I am in a lot of pain.

It takes me three years,
I'm able to stand,
I'm back in,
And I'm feeling better than ever.

I have relearnt gymnastics
And I'm better than ever.

Seren Conway (13)
Flint High School, Flint

Me And My Brother Fin

There was pounding at the door, people barging in,
They were tearing up our house, looking for me and Fin,
All I could hear was my mother screaming,
"No, please stop, don't take my babies in!"
It was too late,
I was sold to a plantation 500 miles away from Fin,
Not feeling confident in my own skin,
I was only seven and spoke a different language,
So I did not fit in.
I was tired of being treated like something from a bin.
I just wanted to go home and see my mum and Fin.
I tried to escape but no matter what I could not win,
My patience was wearing very thin.
This is your reminder to be kind to everyone within,
And don't treat people like they treated me and my brother Fin.

Seren Thompson (12)
Flint High School, Flint

Paper Poem

I am life or so I think.
I am great.
I'm everything you make.
Water is my worst enemy, he spoils me. He destroys me.
I can be anything you think, so try and make anything.
Anything you like.
I can be an aeroplane, a boat, a model, anything! It's your decision.
But my story is tragic.
I am not like plastic.
How to be me, to start, you cut down a tree.
I am not very special to the world.
Kids rip me without a word.
When I get ripped I die.
Then in the bin is where I lie.
So try anything, I won't care.
I'm not as soft as a bear.
So I will know I'm unimportant.
Kids, they think I am important.
But I am nothing I scream.
Maybe I will be in a dream.

Rhys Messiter (11)
Flint High School, Flint

The Day That The Life I Loved Ended

Three seconds, three minutes, three hours.
How long it had been I could no longer tell.
Blinding lights were flashing in my face.
All I remember is that day.

The day that the life I loved ended.

The wave of civilians rushed me along.
Blue flashing lights sang their repetitive song.
At that moment, I knew that that would be me.
Never did I think about the value of being free.
Oh, how I wish I did.

On the day that the life I loved ended.

A blue transparent gown.
A mask covering my face.
Scalpels and scissors.
On the operating table, I spent my days.

Except on the day that the life I loved ended.

Lila Grace Jordens (12)
Flint High School, Flint

War Soldier

Petrifying, traumatising, fighting in the war,
I have already risked my life, I can't do much more.

Depressed and unhopeful, losing friends on the way,
When I think of my family my tears can't stay away.

Day after day, waiting to attack,
Day after day, waiting to be sent back.

To see my family again after a while,
Would change my face from a frown to a smile.

I must fight for my country and stay courageous and strong,
Now I know this is what I was born to do all along.

Being here and having what it takes,
I'm a hero, that's not a mistake.

Angel Williams (12)
Flint High School, Flint

The Pen And I

What do you see as I sit on your desk?
Do you see a black pen on a table,
Or do you see a short black cable?
I love my pen, it's always by my side,
With ink and paper, my thoughts I can't hide.
Writing stories and dreams, it's so much fun,
The pen and I, together we get things done.
In my hand, the pen takes flight,
Words flowing, pure and bright.
It weaves tales upon the page,
Unlocking new worlds at every stage.
With each stroke, a story is born,
Emotions penned from dusk to morn.
The ink is a vessel for my soul,
The pen, my friend, makes me whole.

Savio Costa (13)
Flint High School, Flint

Criminal's Life

I used to be a child,
Now I don't even smile.

Once I became a teenager I got addicted to crime,
And now I need a lot of help, big time,
All I can do in my spare time is rhyme.

I'm a criminal,
'Cause every time I write a rhyme,
People think it's a crime,
To tell them what's on my mind,
I guess I'm a criminal.

Now, what goes through my mind,
At the time of the vicious crime?

I'm trying to get my life back,
But all I can do is fight back,
When I think about my crimes,
I get flashbacks.

Antonia Moise (12)
Flint High School, Flint

Love What You Love

N ature is something we need to look after
A lways go out and admire the nature around
T hink before you step on and kill that plant
U nite, we can all come together with nature.
R ecycle so we don't have to say goodbye to nature,
E very piece of litter you pick up is worth it.

Love all nature that's around you, it won't last forever.
Wildlife is half of nature that we need to look after.
You are one of the people who can make a difference.
Honour nature while it's here, because it won't always be.

Lloyd Wilkes (13)
Flint High School, Flint

Through Our Eyes

At first we didn't know what to think
Maybe they were coming to help us? Or to hurt us?
We hoped they were nice and friendly
We also hoped we would become friends

But we couldn't understand what they were saying
They were bringing factory equipment, their belongings
They were attacking some of our friends and family

I felt powerless, they took away our children
I angrily wiped away my tears and the war began
They killed a few of our friends and family
But that didn't stop us, we were determined to get our land back.

Lexi-Ann O'Brien
Flint High School, Flint

Ghost

In the moonlit night, a ghost appears,
Silent and delicate filled with ancient fear,
Through the mist, it glides, a whisper in the air,
Haunting the shadows everywhere.

Its presence is felt, though it can't be seen,
A spirit invisible but forever keen.
It lingers in the darkness, a spectral delight,
A ghostly figure stalking in the night.

With each passing breeze, it whispers its tale,
Of lost souls and secrets, beyond the earthly veil.
So, let us embrace the ghostly unknown,
And marvel at the mysteries it has shown.

Ethan Williams (14)
Flint High School, Flint

Wales

I am a woman brave and strong
I saw Wales, lovely and bronze
Shining sun sometimes rain
I just want to see the trains.

Amazing beaches, shining sea
I just want to run so free
Nice tall mountains cover the sky
I just like the foggy vibe.

I am a woman with a proud heart
Who just made the world start
Roses pose across the green
I'm one who just wants the Earth clean
So we can make the world breathe.

I am a woman
And I love Wales
It's such a beautiful place to be
For a woman like me.

Scarlett Thompson (12)
Flint High School, Flint

Unhuman

Unnoticed, unseen, don't be scared of me.
Terrible, frightful and grim I might be,
But no need to be scared of me.

I'm eerie and uncanny,
But no need to be scared of me.

Ghastly, unearthly, informal and spooky,
No need to be scared of me.

No matter where or when, I'll still be unseen.
No matter who or what, I'll still be no one.
No need to be worried about me.

Or scared, or sad, or panicked about me.
I'll still be here at the end of the day.
Alone and sad with nobody to scare.

Cerys Holt (11)
Flint High School, Flint

Freedom

In the beginning, we were utterly confused,
Were they friendly or were they nasty?
But we tried for friendship and a free place.
We thought they were nice and came for freedom with not many.
They stole our land and our silver and gold.
They stole our homes and our futures.
There were too many of them we never stood a chance against them.
At first, we were devastated, destroyed and depressed.
We were left upset and almost homeless.
Our tears were dropping so we just sat there before sunset.
But now we are angry and want to fight back.

Dylan Jones (23)
Flint High School, Flint

Alone And Confused

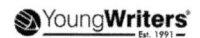

Alone and confused,
Things I wish I had refused,
People say we're just animals,
Say we have no feelings,
But we do, you just can't see them.
People leave us outside on the coldest nights,
Leave us to shiver and leave us in fright
While they're upstairs having a chill night.
So, look after all animals,
Especially the ones you welcome into your home.
When they treat me right,
It's just for a day, just a phase,
They gave me a treat and think that's enough.
No, they are just rough.

Ryan Gittins (13)
Flint High School, Flint

Freedom

In the beginning, we didn't know what to think.
Were they friendly or were they enemies?
We hoped for friendship and freedom.
I was unfazed by their arrival.

They started to take our country.
They took our land.
We hoped they were kind and free.
They began to destroy our homes, our land and our nature.
Steal from us.

They stole our land, our homes and our futures.
They killed our family.
It was like a war zone.
Death and destruction were everywhere.
We didn't stand a chance.

Muhib Ansari
Flint High School, Flint

Overthinker

As I am here loud and clear,
I stand at the front for everyone to hear,
Everyone was quiet, quiet like a mouse,
When I spoke my words no words came out.
I stood there in silence when people watched me shiver,
The crowd was just getting bigger and bigger,
I tried, I tried, I tried so hard,
But all my thoughts were just getting quicker,
I guess that's what you get
For being an overthinker.
You are lost for words,
And care what people think,
But do people really care about
Every little thing?

Lexie Butcher (13)
Flint High School, Flint

I Love My Job

I wake up to see my phone blowing up, I love my friends.
They're the reason I still go on.
My name is Hannah Lowther, and I love my job.
When I get there it all hits me, the adrenaline,
Getting ready is so much fun.
Making new friends that I spend all my time with.
The thrill of hearing the music start is incredible.
But the best part is hearing my fans cheering for me.
I love meeting my fans at the stage door,
It's like meeting new people at the end of the day,
That's why I love my job.

Nancy Wilson (13)
Flint High School, Flint

Fading Hope

As I hear the high-pitched sirens again,
I know the routine,
I wish this would end.
I'm scared for my mum,
I'm scared for my dad,
Thinking of the things I once had.
I miss my sister,
They took her away,
Watched my house burn up in flames.
Can anyone or anything stop this never-ending nightmare?
So much has been lost,
We should give in.
I had one ticket to escape,
That I gave to my sister
Who always made my day.
I constantly wonder,
Will we meet again?

Eva Jones (12)
Flint High School, Flint

I Am A Flower

I am a flower swaying in the air,
I am colourful and bright yet they don't care.

Sitting in the ground with people passing by,
All I see day and night is the black and blue sky.

I want to be noticed and use my time,
So I'm going to spread and find walls to climb.

That is how I want to use my time,
Maybe I'm worthless only worth a dime.

Possibly not even that,
I'm worthless anyway, I will only end up stamped on and become all flat...

Carys Fion Williams (12)
Flint High School, Flint

A Strand Of Hair

Here I am, a strand of hair,
And I think my life is really unfair.
I'm straightened and straightened at eight on the dot,
The plates are like lava, this is just too hot.
She bleaches me and strips me of colour, causing split ends,
And puts me in curlers so my body then bends.

Just when I think she will leave me alone,
She cuts me in half, right down to the bone.
I get drowned in the shower, I get wetter and wetter,
Oh, I wish my hard life would get a bit better!

Maizie Jones (13)
Flint High School, Flint

Imprisoned Hope

Desperate for freedom
You are confined alone
Stuck with no escape
Trying to escape but it never works
Only wish we could be free
Preyed on like an animal
In pain from the beating
Always worried and scared
Never happy, never joyful
Scared of what might happen
Alone and horrified, I wish someone could help
Can't get out, can't be free
I wish a miracle could happen
End the suffering
Time to come, let's hope
You and me will be free.

Kian Taylor (14)
Flint High School, Flint

A Dog's Perspective

As I wake up in the morning to the smell of kibble
As my owner gets ready for this day
As she sets off for school, I sleep for a good 6 hours
As I see my person I light up in excitement
As I rush to her I must go to the toilet so I don't have any accidents before our walk
As I stomp through the field of uncut grass and the fallen crispy leaves I spot a new friend and rush over
As we finally get home I have a quick bath as it is already very late and I've already fallen asleep.

Evie Ross (13)
Flint High School, Flint

A Rucksack's Travel

The air grows thinner as we ascend further
Our horizons getting foggier
My contents rustling with the steep steps
Snow begins swirling and encircling
Making it oh so cold
The peak seems so close and yet it's so far
They reach a tall, stony cliff
To continue we'd have to climb
I feel my arms slip off of the shoulder of my owner
He stops to fix the straps but his arm slips off
I feel my other strap fall
And I feel myself hit the floor.

Flynn Osborne (12)
Flint High School, Flint

The Sound That Lurks

It's too dark, derelict and dicey
To construct an ark
To decamp this maze
Though dear, don't you fear, we will escape this disgrace
Promise me if you overhear a creak, do not peek!
What you get a glimpse of may make you squeak
Be aware that the bangs, bashes and crashes
Perhaps give the most sinister out-of-body experience
Or the spine-chilling uninvited visitor
That lurks and watches you through the lenses
That aren't your glasses.

Efe Igbinoba (14)
Flint High School, Flint

The Raging Fire

I start as a small, little ember carried by the wind
But I find my home on the side of a bright green tree
And start eating my way through the serene Amazon rainforest

I stomp my way flowing with the wind
When more obstacles come I burn them to ashes
And leave nothing behind
On the horizon

I see some people alongside my worst nightmare
I push my way through
But my downfall has arrived
I am put out to an ember once again.

Adam Mrlina (12)
Flint High School, Flint

Teeth

T oothpaste, I am crucial to life.
O rthodontist gives you a fright.
O ne more cavity could appear overnight.
T wice a day, it's all you need.
H appy and amazed, with your shiny teeth.
P ower of toothpaste never had a doubt.
A ll of our teeth, thank me!
S uperbrands all for your teeth.
T oothbrush and toothpaste, best duo out there.
E very dentist loves me, I am toothpaste.

Hannah Squire (12)
Flint High School, Flint

The Overseer

I come in many forms
I see many things
Sometimes it might be a college dorm
Or it could be the great outdoors
Where it looks very nice
Could be hot or filled with ice
But I don't mind
I see great sights
I definitely prefer this over the other kind.

Sometimes I watch over things
Of great importance
Sometimes I am a bit pointless
Nevertheless, I do my job
Although I am only a camera bought from the shop.

Osian Jones (14)
Flint High School, Flint

A Lost Refugee

Intimidating and frightening but I must stay strong,
I knew I would have to do this all along.

Move away from the place I know and love,
I miss looking at the stars above.

Smoke fills up the skies,
I wish I could make people realise.

I'd rather be anywhere else right now,
I want to escape this place but I don't know how.

It is different and hard to fit in,
But I know this is a fight we can win.

Anna Austin (12)
Flint High School, Flint

The Hero By The City

Strutting around the city lives a lion protecting its pack
Proud, powerful, possibly strong, that's what they say about me
I will stay strong no matter what because I'm the hero of the city
What happens if the villains are stronger than me?
What if it's putting my family and friends at risk?
What happens if the villain is someone I know?
The villain might have a really sad life story
I'm a hero and I'll try my best.

Kendal Cohen (11)
Flint High School, Flint

Why Am I The Villain?

Strong, sharp and steady, proudly prowling around New York,
Fear on other people's faces as they stare at me.

Mean, nasty and horrible, that's what everyone says about me.
Why am I the villain?

Hiding all of my tattoos with my blazer, hiding the truth about me
Making traps around me so I can catch people

Hiding in the shadows, scaring people as they're passing by
They will all bow down to me one day.

Keeva Beck (12)
Flint High School, Flint

Life Of A Refugee

Lost once again,
Falling out of bed
From the gunfire
By the shed.
Bombs and no sound around,
Everyone running around,
But no one around.

Life falling apart like
The houses around,
Infantry around,
Can't get out!
Face-to-face with a bomb,
Get out!
Eating me alive, *get down!*

Life lost,
No one to get me home again.
Anything to get me home again.

Jack Collins (12)
Flint High School, Flint

Through Historical Eyes

At the time they were controlled by one power
British Settlement of Australia
Being a penal colony
Governed by a captain of the Royal Navy.

Controlled by one people is power over another.

A practice of policy of control by establishing colonies
They took over land
Our future in life.

They took our family
Our life and our land
They killed most of our men in the war
And they stole our money.

Kacey-Leigh Jones (13) & Katie
Flint High School, Flint

The Snowflake

When I start to appear,
That is when you know that winter is here.
My crystal-like body lets off a glow,
I glow proudly in the thick of the snow.
I fall proudly down to the floor,
When people see they look up at the sky to see one.

When people spot me they see me up high,
Gliding through the snowy sky.
But when spring comes around,
I stay on the ground.
Once I have melted I'm nowhere to be found.

Brody Duncan (13)
Flint High School, Flint

The Busy Ball

The crowd cheers as I glide in the air,
Ferocious kicking, making me scared.
Up and down from left to right,
I can't stand this vicious sight.
The crowd goes wild, cheering, "Goal!"
I don't know what's happening, I'm just a ball.

The sun is shining and the stadium is bright,
Players shouting as I take flight.
Hot to cold, left to right,
I'm quite enjoying this great sight.

Riley Smith (13)
Flint High School, Flint

Lights, Camera, Action!

I have a cat.
And a gnat.
My mask hides my face.
I always win the race.
They call me when no heroes are around.
One second they're there and then never to be found.
I'd swear it wasn't me.
I wish they'd leave me be.
I try to hide my face,
Before they begin the chase.
I am a shadow, as swift as can be,
Haunting the night, they will all bow to me.
Ready or not, here I come!

Olivia Marsh (12)
Flint High School, Flint

Me

Hiding your feelings is a tough thing to do,
But it can be for a good reason too.
Always being happy isn't easy,
While you walk around feeling queasy.

Sometimes you feel like you can't speak your truth,
And that you just gotta push through.

Your thoughts are your monsters,
And your pain is your pride.
But your true self slowly dies inside,
While you wait for what's ahead.

Emily Seddon (12)
Flint High School, Flint

Water Is Calm

Imagine you are water in the ocean,
Not a care in the world and no commotion.
It's just you, the fish and the sun,
No jobs or chores, nothing needs to be done.

Just go with the flow and travel the Earth,
Go out there and see it, you'll know its worth.

I know this poem was quite short but to bring it to an end,
I have one last thing to say,

Be like water, my friend.

Thomas Latham (12)
Flint High School, Flint

The Best Dogs In My Life

My dogs are the best dogs ever
Because they fight for their life
Fight off rats
And they are really good at tricks
But one day my dog Pepper got Covid
And she died, but we got another dog
Called Kitty
And she is a German shepherd crossed
With a husky.
Kitty was a puppy when we got her
And now she is so tall
And she plays with me
And she is just the best.

Darcel Jones (12)
Flint High School, Flint

Snowflake

S now is my mother,
N ow I am free,
O nce a bit of snow,
W ow! I've become more,
F or every winter I always fall,
L ovingly placing myself on a child's coat,
A child always makes me into a snowman,
K eeping me there is hard because one day I will vanish,
E ating me up is the rain and I am gone. *Poof!*

Chelsea Collo (12)
Flint High School, Flint

School

People come in and out every day,
On the same days even at the same times,
No one ever stays,
People are good, they are gone,
I wished they'd stay,
If I ever made a friend,
They're not here to stay,
Just a few years,
Then they're gone,
Every day I think they're going,
Just like the year 11s,
I'm so scared they're not coming back.

Olivia Owens (11)
Flint High School, Flint

Flower In The Rain

I love summer!
It's so warm and sunny!
I feel so colourful and healthy.
All good things come to an end though.
I hate winter.
I never have any friends, I'm all alone.
I look around and the grass is grey.
I look for my friend but there is nothing to see.
I will die in the rain.
I always feel old and grey.
Summer will come soon though.
Very soon.

Lola Hammersley (11)
Flint High School, Flint

What Soldiers Do For Us

Soldiers fight for us.
Soldiers die for us.
Soldiers kill for us.
And what do we do?
Nothing.

Soldiers are brave.
Soldiers are strong.
Soldiers are ready.
And what do we do?
Nothing.

Soldiers would save us.
Would you save us?
Soldiers would risk their lives.
Would you?
Soldiers would do anything.
What would you do?

Caelan Acott (13)
Flint High School, Flint

Criminal

Once I was a boy,
And now I just annoy.
Am I just a criminal?
Or am I just invincible?

Reflections pass through my mind,
Reflections of my happy life.
My words are like a dagger with a jagged edge,
It all started when I forgot to cut the hedge.

My crime time,
Is my part-time job.
I've never been caught,
I will never be watched.

Ruby Cowden (11)
Flint High School, Flint

Through Our Eyes

In the beginning we did not know what to think at first
They were friendly, or so we thought...

They looked different to us
They talked different to us
They took our children from us...

They built a fence to keep us out...
But the fence got bigger and bigger...
There was nothing we could do

Sometimes we had fights but they always won...

Juliet Lewis
Flint High School, Flint

The Helpful Hero

H elpful, caring and positive, that's what they say about me.
E ven strutting round the city everyone needs my help.
R unning fast like a cheetah, I save people's lives
O n every rooftop I will look out for my city.
I am the greatest hero to help this city.
C ould I win against the villain? Or would I lose and let my city down?

Hollie Warburton
Flint High School, Flint

Through War-Torn Eyes

At the start we didn't know,
If they were friend or foe.
They came in with ships and boats,
We didn't know who they were.

They broke our homes,
They took our possessions,
Took our hills,
They started war.

They brought their families,
They made us fight,
There was fire and smoke everywhere,
There were too many.

Frankie Price
Flint High School, Flint

Villain Mayhem

V ile, rude, nasty, that's what they call me
I don't get why people hate me
L ife is rough and hard
L ike a fast cheetah, I run from heroes
A lways causing mayhem for this city
I was a bad girl, did some bad things
N ever turn against your family, always be a villain. Life, laugh, love being a villain.

Lexi-May Sebrina McCarron (12)
Flint High School, Flint

Through A Villain's Eyes

Hiding in the shadows, waiting for my prey, making sure no heroes come to save the day
Evil, nasty, horrid, that's what they call me
Powerful, proud, brave, that's what I am
Crawling around like a chameleon, camouflaged into the walls
Maybe I'm not that bad a person after all
Lonely, I wander around, looking for something.

Mia Brown (12)
Flint High School, Flint

Forget

Standing there, watching in horror.
A tear drops down from my eye.
As I watch the soldiers that I befriended slowly die.

I now sit in my house scared to move.
The creaking of the floorboards made me want to hide.
A mouse scurrying made me want to cry.
I wish I could forget.
I wish I could leave the memories behind.

Keira Newton (12)
Flint High School, Flint

Lamppost

In the dark night, a guiding light,
A lamppost stands tall, shining bright.
Stories unfold, dreams take flight,
Underneath its warm, comforting light.

Oh, lamppost, you're more than just a light,
You bring warmth and magic to the night.
A symbol of hope, a familiar sight,
A lamppost shining with all its might.

Finley Russell (13)
Flint High School, Flint

Darkness Consumes Me

I am powerful, positive and strong.
Kind, helpful and happy. That's what the kids say about me.
Spying the city for villains. As the darkness hides me.
I save people, I'm not dangerous.
Hidden in the darkness. Looking for villains.
As I see the villains, I think to myself,
Am I doing the correct thing?

Calvin Peters (11)
Flint High School, Flint

Bored Killer

Destroying buildings is the only fun thing to do.

(Although I like pizza)

The other day I went to Korea to kill the Korean president,
He was not there, so I came back.

Some buildings were full of police, so I destroyed them
But the X-Men were there,
There was a green guy that looked like a pear...

Luis Griffith (12)
Flint High School, Flint

Lake

I'm always awake,
Maybe not all clean,
But still calm and slow.
Someone made me dirty today, however
It was a calm part,
So it didn't affect me too much.
The life of me is always,
Always calm and soothing,
But people sometimes don't understand
How easy and peaceful a life can be.

Callum Harding (12)
Flint High School, Flint

Princess Sofia

P rincess Sofia the First
R eady to take over the throne
I n this humongous palace what a way to live
N ever give up
C arrying my tiaras to the shelf
E veryone loves the way I rule the palace
S uccessful and happy is the way to live
S uch a great life.

Sophia Jones (11)
Flint High School, Flint

Confusion

Frustrated and confused
I didn't know what to lose
I got in an altercation with Klopp
For being sidelined
I used to get told, "You'll never make it."
Didn't let that stop me, I kept going
This world is a mess
We're losing 2-1
I'm different to the rest.

Leon Croll (12)
Flint High School, Flint

Rosa Parks

As I look at the white person,
Telling me to move because she thinks she's better,
I protest, telling her I'm just the same as her,
Telling the bus driver I should be treated the same,
But no, I get put in jail for the lack of my rights and
For any other black person in this cruel world.

Nia-Jane Hinds (13)
Flint High School, Flint

Villain

V icious, vile and victorious
I will win and never fall
L ove me or hate, I do not care
L ike me or not, you will all stare
A nd you will bow down
I will rule, not a care in the world
N ever will you know whose face hides under the crown.

Olivia Marsh (12)
Flint High School, Flint

My Mum

My mum, the best person on Earth, working so hard to care for us.
Wishing I could help her work but I'm still young.
You and me, best friends forever, knowing I am going to love you forever.
Upset a lot but not alone because when I speak to my mum she makes me my own.

Carla Showell (12)
Flint High School, Flint

Homeless

H omeless person
O ut on the street
M oney is a big problem
E vacuated from my own home
L ost and don't know how
E mbarrassed I am
S oggy clothes and
S obbing myself to sleep every night.

Anthony Smith (12)
Flint High School, Flint

Wheelchair

My wheelchair is my legs,
Without it, I would be stuck,
My chair has brought me confidence,
It's even brought me luck!

I can get from A to B,
Or even C to D,
I can go fast or slow,
Wherever you want me to be.

Ryan Lally (12)
Flint High School, Flint

Nigeria

First they said they would trade
But then they betrayed
They came in through the land
They pillaged the villages
Then the cities before
They became rubble
Just like our country that crumbled
To the British Empire.

Ethan Thomas (12)
Flint High School, Flint

Winter

People love all the seasons,
But they don't love me.
I love seeing people in mittens,
I love seeing children play in my snow.

Stamping feet, saying brrr,
I am king this time of year.

Grace Jones (13)
Flint High School, Flint

Love

L onging for love every day.
O n and on in people's heads all day.
V ery precious moments lie ahead.
E verything exciting waiting to begin.

Evie Hale (12)
Flint High School, Flint

A Mother's Love

I am a therapist
I am a hugger
I am a daughter
I am a sister
I am a chef
I am strong
I am a bedtime reader
I am a mother.

Penelope Ann Machell (11)
Flint High School, Flint

A Glass Of Water

Sometimes life is
like a glass of
water.
Don't add any
more water to the
glass if you don't know
how to clean it up.

Millie Roberts (13)
Flint High School, Flint

Heroic Heroism

H owever crime happens, I stop it
E veryone loves me
R esilience is my main thing
O ver rooftops I run.

Alex Doran (12)
Flint High School, Flint

My Life As A River

I started as a raindroplet, landing on the mountain
I joined the other rain droplets and we started our journey down the mountain
Halfway down the mountain we joined a fast-flowing stream
Which made our journey much faster

The roller coaster of a stream sent us rocking left and right
Along the journey we picked up some mud and rocks
Which we dragged down the rest of the mountain
The rocks scraped against the bank of the river
Making the stream wider

We made it down to the bottom of the mountain
And joined a super, big river heading for the ocean
Which I think the humans call a canal

Our journey was almost finished
We made our way to the mouth of the river
Where we joined the sea
And I started my second journey all around the world
Where I went to China, America and Antarctica
And then it all started again in a cloud.

Martha Neininger (12)
Gloucester Academy, Gloucester

People's Opinions

Having your own opinion is okay,
Just keep them to yourself or they'll get to you,
Because they say, "A fish who keeps its mouth shut never gets caught."
You don't need to agree with other's opinions,
But be kind and respect them.
Don't care about what they say,
Care about what you think about yourself,
And let go of the ones who hurt you,
Let go of the words they hurl your way as you're walking out the door.
And try to hold onto child-like whims,
And moonlight swims,
And you're blazing self-respect.
And don't worry your pretty little mind,
Because people throw rocks at ones that shine.

Joanna Rajah (11)
Gloucester Academy, Gloucester

A Soldier

A t midnight the first gunshots were fired.

S oldiers rose as we gazed towards the horizon.

O ver the mountains we were ambushed by the Russian soldiers.

L ives were lost that day, many of my friends and comrades died to save many innocent people.

D ays went by and still war commenced near my head. I was petrified.

I was finally allowed away from war but I was still jumpy by all the sudden noises that I heard.

E veryone frightened me as I was still adjusting to normal life.

R ight as I was adjusting, the war ended and my days at war still haunt me till the end of my days.

Edward Williamson-Giles (12)
Gloucester Academy, Gloucester

Through The Eyes Of A River

As I charge through the country, I see so much.
If only it could be peaceful.

Being a river would sound quite pleasant,
But if I'm honest, it's anything but.

Always raging, never stopping,
A constant cycle gets so exhausting.

Smashing, crashing, against all the rocks,
I am home to many things and yet I feel so empty.

I seem so beautiful.
But ugly, I really am.
Lives, believe it or not, have been lost at my hands.

Life is crazy, chaotic and cruel,
But one day, one day there will be a peaceful day for me, the river.

George Brooksbank-Hardacre (12)
Gloucester Academy, Gloucester

Abandoned Terrier

They dumped me on the side of the road at only a few weeks old.
I was now just a stray Yorkshire terrier, all alone, waiting for a miracle.

I wandered the big and busy streets of London,
Watching all of the people carelessly rampage past me.

It was only a few months of me wandering the alleys and avenues until a miracle happened.

My new owner, Jacob, saw me scavenging for some sort of food in rubbish bins.
He picked me up and took me in with all of his care.
My life had finally found a place in this world.
I was no longer a stray Yorkshire terrier.

Riley Holpin (12)
Gloucester Academy, Gloucester

Cat In My Yard

C an you imagine being a cat?
A re you interested? Well, you've come to the right feline.
T he way you can be as elegant as me.

I s to be silent, childish and goofy as can be.
N ow my first target is this backyard.

M ove as silently as possible evading the guard.
Y ou see that dog huddled up in his cage

Y ou need to be silent and not make a sound.
A s if you do you'll wake the hound.
R un quickly, and snatch all the treats.
D o make haste we need to retreat.

Luke Butt (12)
Gloucester Academy, Gloucester

Olivia Rodrigo's Genre

Why did it have to be me?
I just want to be free
Love goes back and forth
I just want to be down on Earth
I feel so sad
All because he was so bad
I'm so alone
But I really should have known
I just wanted love
But he was never my beloved
He made me feel insecure
And like a total failure
But obviously it can't be because my life is wicked
Why do I have to be left in the dust?
When it's over they always look at me with disgust
They knew me as Olivia Rodrigo
Now it's just as their ego.

Martha Jones (12)
Gloucester Academy, Gloucester

Luna Lovegood

L ove magical creatures
U nder amazement all the time
N ever going to give up
A lways a strange life

L iving in a hut full
O f crazy
V ery keen to go on adventures
E very day there is something new to do
G ood things come my way
O dd is what they call me
O bviously, I don't care
D efinitely the best.

Aaliyah Knights (11)
Gloucester Academy, Gloucester

The Great One Before Me

I am racing on the track, I can smell it, the rubber burning.
I can hear it, *pop, pop, bang, bang,*
The engine sounding through the exhaust pipe.
I can feel it, the struggle of the steering wheel
Fighting back as I try to turn.
My neck is hurting, the G-force of the speed, it is overwhelming.
I don't think my neck can take it anymore.
Finally, I see it, the finishing line!
Closer and closer,
I've made it!
The cheers of the crowd are inspirational,
"He's made it, number seven has crossed the finish line," the commentator says.
I can see it, the steps of glory.
I am climbing the steps now, one by one,
Each step I climb, I feel like I am getting lighter.
I make it to the top, finally,
Finally!
I have made it to the top of the podium.
I grasp the trophy in my hands.
I now know what it is like for every great racing driver that has stood here.

Kairon Booker (13)
Maple Medical PRU, Balby

My Boy

A young boy from Doncaster,
Loves basketball,
Tackled mid-air,
Snapped ankle,
The hospital spotted something worrying,
It wasn't followed up.

A year later,
Pain and swelling built,
Trousers cut off, this wasn't right,
Doctors said possibly arthritis or blood clot,
A&E was needed,
Top consultants were called,
Didn't know what it was,
A blood clot or...
Lumbar punctures, scans, biopsies, CTs and MRIs.

Days later, the consultant told us,
My boy had cancer,
Birmingham Hospital via ambulance,
More scans,
More specialists,
Cancer confirmed,
Ewing's sarcoma,
My world feels like it is over,
Why has my boy been diagnosed with
Ewing's sarcoma?

Kian Flint (14)
Maple Medical PRU, Balby

I'm Sorry

"I'm sorry,"
It's dark... so dark!
No one will save me, will they?
It's okay, it's warm.
The silence is suffocating.

"I'm sorry,"
It's grey, there's no colour... it's so sad,
A violin plays with a piano,
Graceful and elegant, but rough and painful,
Is someone there? Have they come to save me?

"I'm so sorry...
It was an accident!
Please, don't hate me!"

It's bright, nothing but white for miles,
It's gone.
A hand held out? It's so welcoming.
"It's okay, I'm here now."

Mia Martin (14)
Maple Medical PRU, Balby

Speak Out

I sit in silence,
Feeling scared and sad,
But nobody notices.
Feels like the whole world is on my shoulders,
Always worrying about what will come next.

The room is too quiet,
My thoughts are too loud,
I lie in bed, wide awake, wanting the thought to subside.
Stop! Stop! I want to get off this horrible ride,
I feel sick with fear.
My heart's beating rapidly,
My hands have gone numb,
I want to speak, but the words get trapped.

Evie Lakin (12)
Maple Medical PRU, Balby

The Final Day

I awake,
Mud drenched into my fur,
I wander around this cold, muddy despair.
It hurts.
I wish I could escape!
But they all seem to tearfully smile at me.
Then I see some of them leave and never return,
It hurts!
They all start to scream and panic,
As a yellow gas fills the air.
It consumes us.
It hurts,
I curl up in a corner,
I close my eyes,
For the last time.

Sian Machin (14)
Maple Medical PRU, Balby

Darcey

D estructive
A dmirable
R ambunctious
C apable
E xcited
Y outhful

I am Darcey the horse.

Brooke Woodward (13)
Maple Medical PRU, Balby

YOUNG WRITERS INFORMATION

We hope you have enjoyed reading this book — and that you will continue to in the coming years.

If you're a young writer who enjoys reading and creative writing, or the parent of an enthusiastic poet or story writer, do visit our website **www.youngwriters.co.uk**. Here you will find free competitions, workshops and games, as well as recommended reads, a poetry glossary and our blog. There's lots to keep budding writers motivated to write!

If you would like to order further copies of this book, or any of our other titles, then please give us a call or order via your online account.

Young Writers
Remus House
Coltsfoot Drive
Peterborough
PE2 9BF
(01733) 890066
info@youngwriters.co.uk

Join in the conversation!
Tips, news, giveaways and much more!

- YoungWritersUK
- YoungWritersCW
- youngwriterscw
- youngwriterscw